B. C. Cave In

Johnny Hart

CORONET BOOKS
Hodder Fawcett, London

Copyright © 1967, 1968 by Publishers Newspapers Syndicate
Copyright © 1973 by Fawcett Publications Inc.

First published in 1969 by Fawcett Publications Inc.

Coronet edition 1975
Fifth impression 1981

_____

Printed in Great Britain for Hodder Fawcett, Ltd,
Mill Road, Dunton Green, Sevenoaks, Kent.
(Editorial Office: 47 Bedford Square, London, WC1 3DP)
by Hunt Barnard Printing Ltd
Aylesbury, Bucks

ISBN 0 340 19873 7

10·26

BEEP

11·13

11·17

11·18

AAARRGGHHH

nat

11·20

SMACKO

11·22

ZANG

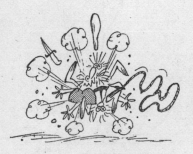

11.23

11·24

11.28

hart

12·5

2.25

1.3

1-23

1·24

.....THIS "OLD FASHIONED"
TASTES FUNNY, DID YOU
MUDDLE THE FRUIT?

1·25

YES.

1·26

1·27

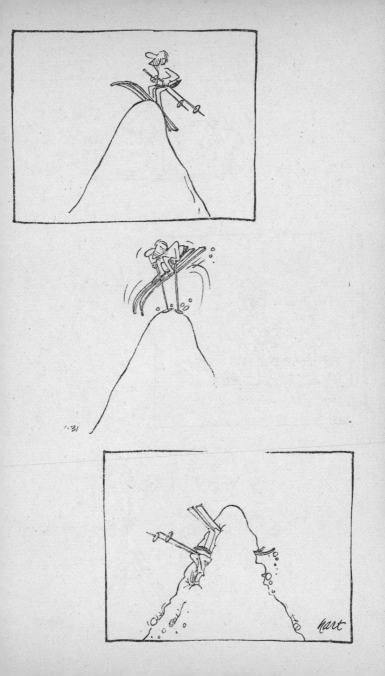

2·1

2·2

2-6

2·7

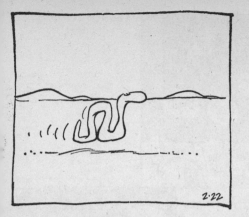

2-22

3·13

nart

3-14

3-25

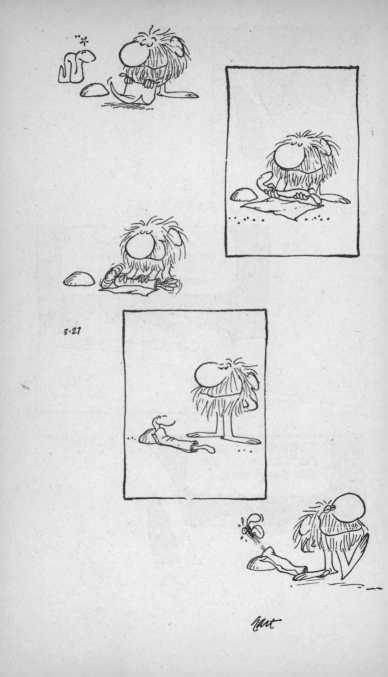

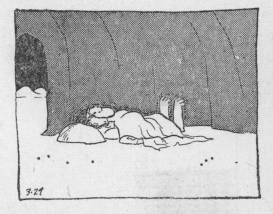

3.29

5·17

5-28

PICK

6·10

SLICE

I CAN'T FIGURE OUT WHY I'M SO UNPOPULAR
..MAYBE IF I HAD A WINNING SMILE... AND MY TONGUE WASN'T FORKED.....
6·24
AND HAD LEGS.... ...AND ARMS... ...AND HAIR.... AND A BIG CHEST .. ...AND... ..
COME TO THINK OF IT, ... IT'S NOT REALLY THAT HARD TO FIGURE OUT
hart

7·10

7-2

hart

8.30

LOOK, LENNY, THEY GOT INSECTS.

9·10

Roast DOOKEY BIRD

CLEAN and DRESS ONE 10lb. BIRD.

9·13

PUCK

9.14

ICE HOCKEY.

9-18

hart

B.C. IT'S A FUNNY WORLD

JOHNNY HART

☐	20653 5	B.C. One More Time	75p
☐	19474 X	B.C. Right On	75p
☐	16881 1	What's New B.C.	75p
☐	18780 8	B.C. Is Alive and Well	75p
☐	15694 5	Hey B.C.!	75p
☐	20762 0	B.C. It's A Funny World	60p
☐	16477 8	Back to B.C.	75p

JOHNNY HART AND BRANT PARKER

☐	16476 X	The Peasants Are Revolting	60p
☐	16899 4	Remember The Golden Rule	75p
☐	25679 7	Wizard Of Id Charge	65p
☐	18604 6	There's A Fly In My Swill	75p

All these books are available at your local bookshop or newsagent, or can be ordered direct from the publisher. Just tick the titles you want and fill in the form below.

Prices and availability subject to change without notice.

CORONET BOOKS, P.O. Box 11, Falmouth, Cornwall.

Please send cheque or postal order, and allow the following for postage and packing:

U.K. – 40p for one book, plus 18p for the second book, and 13p for each additional book ordered up to a £1.49 maximum.

B.F.P.O. and EIRE – 40p for the first book, plus 18p for the second book, and 13p per copy for the next 7 books, 7p per book thereafter.

OTHER OVERSEAS CUSTOMERS – 60p for the first book, plus 18p per copy for each additional book.

Name ....

Address ....

....